Best Wishes,

The Book of All-American Wisdom

Common Sense and Uncommon Genius
From 101 Great Americans

Compiled and Edited by Criswell Freeman

© 1994 by WALNUT GROVE PRESS

All rights reserved. No part of this book may be reproduced or transmitted in any form or by any means, electronic or mechanical, including photocopying, recording, or by information storage or retrieval system, without permission in writing from the publisher.

WALNUT GROVE PRESS
P.O. Box 58128
Nashville, TN, 37205
(615) 320-9128

ISBN 0-9640955-2-1

The ideas expressed in this book are not, in all cases, exact quotations, as some have been edited for clarity and brevity. In all cases, the author has attempted to maintain the speakers' original intent. In some cases, material for this book was obtained from secondary sources, primarily print media. While every effort was made to ensure the accuracy of these sources, that accuracy cannot be guaranteed. For additions, deletions, corrections or clarifications in future editions of this text, please write WALNUT GROVE PRESS.

WALNUT GROVE PRESS books are available at special discounts for sales in bulk purchases, fund-raising, or educational use. For information, contact WALNUT GROVE PRESS.

Printed in the United States of America
by Douglas Printing, Inc.

Book Design by Armour&Armour
Cover Design by Mary Mazer

1 2 3 4 5 6 7 8 9 10 • 94 95 96

ACKNOWLEDGMENTS
The author gratefully acknowledges the helpful support of Angela Beasley, June Bowen, Mary Freeman, Mary Jo Freeman, J. R. Freeman, Steve Parker, Don Pippen, Betty Schnitzer, and George Schnitzer.

To My Grandparents

Virginia and Bill Criswell,
Marie and Harvey Freeman

American Wisdom At Its Best

Table of Contents

Introduction	3
Chapter 1: Yourself	5
Chapter 2: Other People	15
Chapter 3: Experience	23
Chapter 4: Life	31
Chapter 5: Opportunity	39
Chapter 6: Success	45
Chapter 7: Courage	53
Chapter 8: Happiness	61
Chapter 9: Honesty	71
Chapter 10: Education	79
Chapter 11: Freedom	87
Chapter 12: Action	95
Chapter 13: Wisdom	105
Chapter 14: Hope	113
Chapter 15: Change	121
Chapter 16: Your Work	129
Chapter 17: Love and Forgiveness	135
Chapter 18: All Purpose Advice	141
Sources	149

Introduction

For almost 20 years, I've had a hobby. I collect gems of wisdom on 3x5 cards. After two decades of collecting, I decided that the wisdom stored away in my file boxes was too important to keep to myself, so I've compiled some of the *very best* ideas into a concise book of American thought.

Herein lies wisdom that is distinctly American. It tells of a story of hope, courage, confidence, and self-reliance, shared through the words of 101 notable men and women.

This is *not* a quote book in the traditional sense. In some cases, I have edited quotations in order to improve clarity (always, of course, retaining the intent of the authors' original words). And, as a practicing Doctor of Clinical Psychology, I have chosen thoughts that reinforce the principles of good mental health. Enjoy a healthy dose of All-American wisdom. And see if you don't agree with me that American wisdom is wonderfully simple — and simply wonderful.

1

Yourself

The Golden Rule. It asks us to treat others as we wish to be treated. For some of us, however, doing unto others isn't the problem; it's what we do unto ourselves that causes trouble. So here's the Reverse Golden Rule:

Treat yourself as you wish to be treated by others.

Give yourself the benefit of the doubt; forgive yourself when you make a mistake; and pat yourself on the back when you do something good. A positive self-image is at the very core of good mental health; so take the advice of these prominent Americans: Give yourself the respect you deserve. After all, if you don't, who will?

Yourself

Love yourself first.

Lucille Ball

All-American Wisdom

Nothing can bring you peace but yourself.
Ralph Waldo Emerson

Too many people overvalue what they're not
and undervalue what they are.
Malcolm Forbes

I think somehow, we learn who we really are
and live with that decision.
Eleanor Roosevelt

Yourself

One face to the world, another at home
makes for misery.

Amy Vanderbilt

No one can wear one face to himself and
another to the multitude without finally
wondering which is true.

Nathaniel Hawthorne

A man cannot be comfortable
without his own approval.

Mark Twain

All-American Wisdom

Nobody can make you feel inferior
          without your consent.
                                  Eleanor Roosevelt

Assume responsibility for the quality
          of your own life.
                                  Norman Cousins

For an impenetrable shield,
          stand inside yourself.
                                  Henry David Thoreau

Yourself

If you would have a faithful servant, and one you like, serve yourself.

Ben Franklin

Count your blessings and let your neighbor count his.

James Thurber

Believe that life is worth living, and your belief will help create the fact.

William James

All-American Wisdom

Explore thyself. Herein are demanded the eye
and the nerve.
Henry David Thoreau

No one can produce great things who is not
thoroughly sincere in dealing with himself.
James Russell Lowell

When one is estranged from oneself,
then one is estranged from others too.
Anne Morrow Lindbergh

Yourself

Choose a self and stand by it.

William James

All-American Wisdom

If you can't imitate him, don't copy him.

Casey Stengel

Yourself

Never follow the crowd.
> *Bernard Baruch*

Don't craze yourself with too much thinking. Just go about your business.
> *Ralph Waldo Emerson*

Think health, eat sparingly, exercise regularly, walk a lot, and think positively about yourself.
> *Norman Vincent Peale*

Think as little as possible about yourself and as much as possible about other people.
> *Eleanor Roosevelt*

2

Other People

Bernard Shulman, an esteemed Chicago psychiatrist, insists that "People are more like dogs than cats." He notes that most cats seem perfectly content to spend countless hours in solitude. Not so with dogs. They constantly seek companionship. We human beings, like our canine counterparts, seem to function best when we're surrounded by a team of supporters. What follows are some ironclad rules for understanding other people and getting along with them.

Other People

Become genuinely interested in other people.

Dale Carnegie

All-American Wisdom

A man wrapped up in himself
    makes a very small package.
                             Ben Franklin

Getting people to like you is merely
    the other side of liking them.
                        Norman Vincent Peale

Be quick to praise.
                             Bernard Baruch

When someone does something good,
    applaud! You'll make two people happy.
                        Samuel Goldwyn

Other People

Never look down on anybody
    unless you're helping him up.
Jesse Jackson

Never criticize someone else until
    you've walked a mile in his moccasins.
Native American Saying

Any fool can criticize, condemn, and complain,
    and most fools do.
Dale Carnegie

All-American Wisdom

Never make fun of religion, politics, race, or mothers.

Mack Sennett

Other People

We are all salesmen.

Charles M. Schwab

All-American Wisdom

The best way to have a friend is to be one.
Ralph Waldo Emerson

The best argument seems
      merely an explanation.
Dale Carnegie

Pay less attention to what men say.
      Just watch what they do.
Andrew Carnegie

Never trouble another for
      what you can do yourself.
Thomas Jefferson

Reach out and touch someone.
A.T. & T. Slogan, 1982

Other People

Don't talk unless you can improve the silence.

New England Saying

3

Experience

American philosopher George Santayana said, "The great difficulty of education is to get experience out of ideas." It would be wonderful if we could learn life's lessons without living them, but that's seldom the case. Usually, we have to make our own mistakes. Experience is a strict, but effective teacher. It's our job to learn life's lessons sooner rather than later; but don't worry — if we miss something, life will gladly teach the lesson again.

And again. And again. . . .

Experience

I am guided by one lamp: experience.
> *Patrick Henry*

Time is a great teacher.
> *Carl Sandburg*

Life is a series of lessons that must be lived to be understood.
> *Ralph Waldo Emerson*

All-American Wisdom

One thorn of experience is worth
 a whole wilderness of warning.
James Russell Lowell

When you get hurt, use it.
Ernest Hemingway

If I had my life to live over, I'd make
 the same mistakes, only sooner.
Tallulah Bankhead

Experience

Use your eyes as if tomorrow
    you would be stricken blind.
Helen Keller

Nature is always hinting at us.
Robert Frost

Every calamity is a spur and valuable hint.
Ralph Waldo Emerson

Failure isn't making a mistake.
    Failure is not cashing in on it.
Elbert Hubbard

All-American Wisdom

Failure isn't falling down. It's staying down.

Mary Pickford

Experience

All life is an experiment. The more experiments you make, the better.
Ralph Waldo Emerson

Do and dare.
Dale Carnegie

There is no failure except in no longer trying.
Elbert Hubbard

All-American Wisdom

The greatest mistake you can make is to be
   continually fearing you will make one.
Elbert Hubbard

Not failure, but low aim, is the crime.
James Russell Lowell

The way to succeed is to
   double your failure rate.
Thomas J. Watson

Experience

Never let the fear of striking out get in your way.

Babe Ruth

4

Life

Life is a once-in-a-lifetime experience. Treasure it. These ideas will help in your treasure hunt.

Life

If you love life, life will love you back.
Artur Rubinstein

The longer I live,
the more beautiful life becomes.
Frank Lloyd Wright

The best way to prepare for life
is to begin to live.
Elbert Hubbard

Write in your heart that every day
is the best day of the year.
Ralph Waldo Emerson

All-American Wisdom

Life is either a daring adventure or nothing.

Helen Keller

Life

Great minds have purposes,
       others have wishes.
Washington Irving

The greatest use of a life is to spend it
       for something that will outlast it.
William James

Dying seems less sad than
       having lived too little.
Gloria Steinem

All-American Wisdom

Time is a circus always packing up and moving away.

Ben Hecht

Life

When life kicks you,
    let it kick you forward.
E. Stanley Jones

Alter your life by altering your attitudes.
William James

Endeavor to live so that when you die,
    even the undertaker will be sorry.
Mark Twain

Life is 10 percent what you make it
    and 90 percent how you take it.
Irving Berlin

All-American Wisdom

Life is what we make it. Always has been. Always will be.

Grandma Moses

Life

It's a very short trip. While alive, live.
> *Malcolm Forbes*

Time is the least thing we have.
> *Ernest Hemingway*

In three words, I can sum up everything
I know about life:
It goes on.
> *Robert Frost*

5

Opportunity

America is a land of opportunity, but there's a hitch: To be of value, opportunity must be recognized and claimed. Why not reach out for your own unclaimed opportunities? After all, if you don't claim them today, someone else might.

Opportunity

A problem is an opportunity in work clothes.
    Henry J. Kaiser

Industry is a better horse to ride than genius.
    Walter Lippmann

There is no security on this earth;
    there is only opportunity.
    Douglas MacArthur

All-American Wisdom

One today is worth two tomorrows.

Ben Franklin

Opportunity

Don't just grab the first thing that comes by...
    know what to turn down.

Will Rogers

Think of what you can do with what there is.

Ernest Hemingway

The best place to succeed is
    where you are with what you've got.

Charles M. Schwab

All-American Wisdom

This time, like all times, is a very good one,
    if we only know what to do with it.
                        Ralph Waldo Emerson

Knowledge of what is possible
    is the beginning of happiness.
                        George Santayana

Take the obvious, add a cupful of brains,
    a generous pinch of imagination,
    a bucketful of courage,
    and bring to a boil.
                        Bernard Baruch

Opportunity

Whether you think you can or think you can't, you're right.

Henry Ford

Never surrender your dreams.

Jesse Jackson

Plant the seeds of expectation in your mind.

Norman Vincent Peale

6

Success

Success is a hard-won thing. It is much more than bulging bank accounts, pretentious possessions, or luxurious living quarters. Success is a way of thinking. Consider what these outstanding Americans have to say about succeeding — and make your plans accordingly.

Success

Success isn't measured by the position
    you reach in life; it's measured by
    the obstacles you overcome.
Booker T. Washington

Success consists in the climb.
Elbert Hubbard

The secret of success is constancy of purpose.
Ben Franklin

All-American Wisdom

It takes 20 years to make an overnight success.

Eddie Cantor

Success

Wealth is not his that has it,
　　　　　but his that enjoys it.

Ben Franklin

Success in business is his who earns a
　　　living pursuing his highest pleasure.

Henry David Thoreau

Blessed is the man who has found his work.

Elbert Hubbard

All-American Wisdom

Being poor is a frame of mind.

Mike Todd

Money is a terrible master but
an excellent servant.

P. T. Barnum

Greed is a terrible thing —
unless you're in on the ground floor.

Yogi Berra

Success

Destiny is not a matter of chance;
    it's a matter of choice.
        William Jennings Bryan

None of my inventions came by accident.
    They came by work.
        Thomas Edison

It is wonderful how much can be done
    if we are always doing.
        Thomas Jefferson

All-American Wisdom

Nothing great was ever achieved without enthusiasm.

Ralph Waldo Emerson

Success

How to succeed: Try hard enough. How to fail: Try too hard.

Malcolm Forbes

7

Courage

Sometimes we face challenges that are troubling, but necessary. What's required is courage. Here are some thoughts on fear and courage from Americans who, like you and me, have known both.

Courage

There can be no courage unless you're scared.
Eddie Rickenbacker

Courage is resistance to fear, mastery of fear, not the absence of fear.
Mark Twain

Courage is fear holding on a minute longer.
George S. Patton

Pray not for safety from danger,
but for deliverance from fear.
Ralph Waldo Emerson

All-American Wisdom

Fear corrupts.

John Steinbeck

Courage

Character cannot be developed in
    ease and quiet. Only through trial and
        suffering is the soul strengthened.
            Helen Keller

Ask yourself, "What's the worst
    that can happen?" Prepare to accept it.
        Then improve upon the worst.
            Dale Carnegie

A great part of courage is
    having done the thing before.
            Ralph Waldo Emerson

You gain strength, courage, and confidence
    every time you look fear in the face.
            Eleanor Roosevelt

All-American Wisdom

Do the thing you fear, and the death of fear is certain.

Ralph Waldo Emerson

Courage

What counts is not the size of the dog
in the fight; it's the size of the fight in the dog.
Dwight D. Eisenhower

The first and great commandment is
don't let them scare you.
Elmer Davis

One man with courage makes a majority.
Andrew Jackson

Self trust is the essence of heroism.
Ralph Waldo Emerson

All-American Wisdom

You can't steal second base if
    you don't take your foot off first.
Mike Todd

We have nothing to fear but fear itself.
Franklin D. Roosevelt

You must do the thing
    you think you cannot do.
Eleanor Roosevelt

Courage

When you get to the end of your rope, tie a knot and hang on.

Franklin D. Roosevelt

8

Happiness

The Declaration of Independence proclaims that men "are endowed by their creator with certain unalienable rights; that among these are life, liberty, and the pursuit of happiness." How do we pursue happiness? The search begins within our own hearts.

Happiness

We create our own happiness.
> *Henry David Thoreau*

Most people are about as happy
as they make up their minds to be.
> *Abraham Lincoln*

Though we travel the world over to find the
beautiful, we must carry it with us
or we find it not.
> *Ralph Waldo Emerson*

All-American Wisdom

Happiness is a habit. Cultivate it.

Elbert Hubbard

Happiness

Don't mistake pleasure for happiness.

Josh Billings

All-American Wisdom

It is neither wealth nor splendor, but tranquility
and occupation which give
happiness.

Thomas Jefferson

True happiness is not attained through
self-gratification but through
fidelity to a worthy cause.

Helen Keller

Happiness lies in the joy of achievement
and the thrill of creative effort.

Franklin D. Roosevelt

A man is what he thinks about all day long.

Ralph Waldo Emerson

Happiness doesn't depend upon who you are
or what you have; it depends
upon what you think.

Dale Carnegie

Happiness

A sad soul can kill you far quicker
than a germ.

John Steinbeck

When one door of happiness closes,
another opens.

Helen Keller

The happiest man is he who learns from nature
the lesson of worship.

Ralph Waldo Emerson

The happiest people are those who do
the most for others.

Booker T. Washington

All-American Wisdom

The best way to cheer yourself up is to cheer up somebody else.

Mark Twain

Happiness

The cost of a thing is the amount of life that must be exchanged for it.
> *Henry David Thoreau*

Few men own their own property. The property owns them.
> *Robert Ingersoll*

It is easy to get everything you want, provided you first learn to do without the things you cannot get.
> *Elbert Hubbard*

All-American Wisdom

Be simple.
Alfred E. Smith

Happiness

God grant me the serenity
to accept the things I
cannot change;
The courage to change
the things I can;
And the wisdom to know
the difference.

Reinhold Niebuhr

9

Honesty

There's an old saying "Honesty is the best policy." Certainly it's important to be honest with other people; but it's just as important (and sometimes much harder) to be honest with ourselves. Here are profound thoughts that will help in the continuing search for the truth, the whole truth, and nothing but the truth.

Honesty

Honesty is the first chapter
        in the book of wisdom.

Thomas Jefferson

Every truth leads to another.

Ralph Waldo Emerson

If the rascals knew the advantages of virtue,
      they would become honest.

Ben Franklin

All-American Wisdom

When in doubt, tell the truth.

Mark Twain

Honesty

If you tell the truth, you don't have to remember what you said.

Mark Twain

Rather than love, than money, than fame, give me truth.

Henry David Thoreau

Be honest with yourself, so you will be honest with others.

Bernard Baruch

All men should strive to learn before they die what they are running from, and to, and why.

James Thurber

All-American Wisdom

Don't compromise yourself. You're all you've got.

Janis Joplin

Honesty

He is less removed from the truth who believes
    nothing than he who believes
        what is untrue.
                Thomas Jefferson

It takes two to speak the truth:
    one to speak and one to hear.
                Henry David Thoreau

Nothing makes a man as mad as the truth.
                Mark Twain

All-American Wisdom

Truth is tough. It will not break.
>	*Oliver Wendell Holmes, Sr.*

He who lends a truth lights a torch.
>	*Robert Ingersoll*

The truth is more important than the facts.
>	*Frank Lloyd Wright*

Honesty

Live truth instead of professing it.

Elbert Hubbard

10

Education

Where does real education begin? It begins with a burning desire for knowledge. If you want to teach, then first kindle the will to learn. And if you want to learn, find something that profoundly interests you. When you do, the education will take care of itself.

Education

An investment in knowledge always pays
 the best interest.
Ben Franklin

Education is what survives after
 what has been learned has been forgotten.
B. F. Skinner

Secure an education at any cost.
Booker T. Washington

A child educated only at school is an
 undereducated child.
George Santayana

Training is everything.
Mark Twain

All-American Wisdom

Read the best books first.

Henry David Thoreau

Education

Learn from everyone.

Ben Franklin

All-American Wisdom

A whale ship was my Yale and my Harvard.
         Herman Melville

Tell me, and I'll forget.
  Show me, and I may not remember.
    Involve me, and I'll understand.
         Native American Saying

The education of a man is completed
  only when he dies.
         Robert E. Lee

Education

The secret of education is respecting the pupil.
Ralph Waldo Emerson

The better part of every man's education
is that which he gives himself.
James Russell Lowell

To be proud of knowledge is to be
blinded by the light.
Ben Franklin

Every scholar is surrounded
by wiser men than he.
Ralph Waldo Emerson

All-American Wisdom

Think.

Thomas J. Watson

Education

You can observe a lot just by watching.

Yogi Berra

11

Freedom

More than two centuries ago, America was founded upon the ideal of individual freedoms; but the concept of freedom, so beautiful in its simplicity, has proven to be more difficult in its implementation. Despite our great strides, the struggle continues. Thomas Jefferson, Abraham Lincoln, and Martin Luther King are gone. Now that struggle is ours.

Freedom

America is a passionate belief in freedom.
Harry Emerson Fosdick

All men are born free and equal, and have certain natural, essential, unalienable rights.
John Adams

Those who expect to reap the blessings of freedom must undergo the fatigue of supporting it.
Thomas Paine

I know not what course others may take, but as for me, give me liberty or give me death.
Patrick Henry

All-American Wisdom

Every generation must wage a new war
for freedom.
Conference for Progressive Political Action, 1924

In its truest sense, freedom cannot be bestowed,
it must be achieved.
Franklin D. Roosevelt

Justice is always in jeopardy.

Walt Whitman

Sell all and purchase liberty.

Patrick Henry

Freedom

Repression is the seed of revolution.
Daniel Webster

Injustice anywhere is a threat to
   justice everywhere.
Martin Luther King, Jr.

There's no freedom on earth for those
   who deny freedom to others.
Elbert Hubbard

All-American Wisdom

What other liberty is worth having
if we have not freedom and peace in our minds?
Henry David Thoreau

All the ills of democracy can be cured
      by more democracy.
Alfred E. Smith

Freedom

I have a dream that my four little children will one day live in a nation where they will not be judged by the color of their skin but by the content of their character.
Martin Luther King, Jr.

The triumph of justice is the only peace.
Robert Ingersoll

All-American Wisdom

Virtue knows no color lines.

Ida B. Wells

Freedom

Freedom is the supreme good —
> freedom from self-imposed limitation.
>> *Elbert Hubbard*

If you cannot be free,
> be as free as you can.
>> *Ralph Waldo Emerson*

Freedom is a habit.

Carl Sandburg

12

Action

In our daily battles, procrastination is the enemy. What's required is action — even when we're afraid. Here is some All-American advice on getting the job done — *now*.

Action

You may delay, but Time will not.

Ben Franklin

All-American Wisdom

Nothing is so fatiguing as the hanging on
of an uncompleted task.

William James

As a cure for worry, work is better than whiskey.

Thomas Edison

He who hesitates is last.

Mae West

Action

When you have a choice and don't make it,
that is, in itself, a choice.
William James

To escape criticism,
do nothing, say nothing, be nothing.
Elbert Hubbard

All-American Wisdom

A problem well-stated is a problem half solved.

Charles Kettering

Action

Be sure you're right —
                then go ahead.
Davy Crockett

Take time to deliberate; but when
       the time for action arrives,
            stop thinking and go on.
Andrew Jackson

Once a decision is reached,
       stop worrying and start working.
William James

All-American Wisdom

Rhetoric is a poor substitute for action.
Teddy Roosevelt

Speak little, do much.
Ben Franklin

Never mistake motion for action.
Ernest Hemingway

Action

The best way out is always through.
Robert Frost

Seize the first opportunity to act upon
every resolution you make.
William James

Industry is a better horse to ride than genius.
Walter Lippmann

All the beautiful sentiments in the world
weigh less than a single lovely action.
James Russell Lowell

Everything comes to him who hustles
while he waits.
Thomas Edison

All-American Wisdom

Above all, try something.

Franklin D. Roosevelt

Action

Today is when everything that's going to happen from now on begins.

Harvey Firestone, Jr.

13

Wisdom

Ben Franklin said, "The Doors of Wisdom are never shut." Despite this open door policy, the current state of world affairs proves that the Halls of Wisdom are not overly crowded. Would you like an extra helping of genius? Take these thoughts to heart. They're guaranteed to carry you right to the Doors of Wisdom — and beyond.

Wisdom

Life is a festival only to the wise.

Ralph Waldo Emerson

All-American Wisdom

The first problem is not to learn,
        but to unlearn.

Gloria Steinem

It's better to know some of the questions
        than to know all of the answers.

James Thurber

It's better to know nothing than to know
        what isn't so.

Josh Billings

Never answer a critic
        unless he's right.

Bernard Baruch

Wisdom

It requires wisdom to understand wisdom;
the music is nothing if the audience is deaf.

Walter Lippmann

A thought is often original though you have
uttered it a thousand times.

Oliver Wendell Holmes, Sr.

What is the hardest thing to do in the world?
To think.

Ralph Waldo Emerson

See the possibilities.

Norman Vincent Peale

All-American Wisdom

Adopt the pace of nature;
      her secret is patience.

Ralph Waldo Emerson

Genius is nothing but a greater aptitude
      for patience.

Ben Franklin

Genius borrows nobly.

Ralph Waldo Emerson

Wisdom

Time given to thought is
    the greatest time saver of all.
                  Norman Cousins

Wisdom is the power that enables us
    to use knowledge.
                  Thomas J. Watson

The years teach much which
    the days never know.
                  Ralph Waldo Emerson

All-American Wisdom

Nine-tenths of wisdom
>is being wise in time.
>>*Teddy Roosevelt*

Reason often makes mistakes,
>but conscience never does.
>>*Josh Billings*

Wisdom

Wisdom is knowing what to overlook.

William James

14

Hope

Hope gives life its flavor. As long as hope lives, so do we; but when hope dies, a piece of the soul dies with it. Here are some helpful hints from some hopeful Americans.

Hope

Hope is a thing with feathers,
    That perches in the soul.
        Emily Dickinson

The future belongs to those who
    believe in the beauty of their dreams.
        Eleanor Roosevelt

The reason for idleness and crime is the
    deferring of our hopes.
        Ralph Waldo Emerson

Keep hope alive.
        Jesse Jackson

All-American Wisdom

Entertain great hopes.

Robert Frost

Hope

The greatest asset of a man, a business,
or a nation is faith.
Thomas J. Watson

It's unfulfilled dreams that keep you alive.
Robert Schuller

All-American Wisdom

Belief in a thing makes it happen.
Frank Lloyd Wright

They can conquer who believe they can.
Ralph Waldo Emerson

Hope

Act as though it were impossible to fail.

Dorthea Brande

All-American Wisdom

Live from miracle to miracle.

Artur Rubinstein

Hope

An inexhaustible good nature
   is one of the most precious gifts of heaven.
Washington Irving

There is a giant asleep within every man.
   When that giant awakes, miracles happen.
Frederick Faust

When we do the best we can,
   we never know what miracles await.
Helen Keller

15

Change

Change is inevitable. To resist it is to invite disappointment and defeat. When we accept change — and use it to our advantage — change becomes an ally rather than an adversary.

Change

All change is a miracle to contemplate, but it is a miracle that is taking place every instant.
Henry David Thoreau

People wish to be settled; but it is only as far as they are unsettled that there is any hope for them.
Ralph Waldo Emerson

Ask the God who made you to keep remaking you.
Norman Vincent Peale

All-American Wisdom

Only in growth, reform, and change,
paradoxically enough, is true security found.
Anne Morrow Lindbergh

Where we stand is not as important as
the direction in which we are moving.
Oliver Wendell Holmes, Jr.

There is no force so powerful
as an idea whose time has come.
Everett Dirksen

Change

To keep our faces toward change and behave like free spirits in the presence of fate is strength undefeatable.

Helen Keller

All-American Wisdom

The only people who don't change
   their minds are incompetent or dead.
Everett Dirksen

Act the part and you will become the part.
William James

Men do change.

John Steinbeck

Change

Even if you're on the right track, you'll get run over if you sit there long enough.

Will Rogers

When you're green you're growing, when you're ripe you rot.

Ray Kroc

All-American Wisdom

When you cease to make a contribution,
          you begin to die.
Eleanor Roosevelt

Age is a case of mind over matter.
    If you don't mind, it doesn't matter.
Jack Benny

You're never too old to become younger.
Mae West

Change

A man is not old until regrets
　　take the place of dreams.
John Barrymore

No matter how long you live, die young.
Elbert Hubbard

16

Your Work

Americans have a lot to say about work. The ideas in this chapter can be summed up as follows:

Rule 1. FIND WORK THAT YOU LOVE

and

Rule 2. DO IT!

Your Work

Work for your soul's sake.

Edgar Lee Masters

All-American Wisdom

Make the work interesting, and
    discipline will take care of itself.
                                          E. B. White

Think enthusiastically about everything,
    especially your work.
                                Norman Vincent Peale

Each man's talent is his call.
    There is one direction in which
        all doors are open to him.
                                Ralph Waldo Emerson

Your Work

Work and save.

Bernard Baruch

When troubles arise,
       wise men go to their work.

Elbert Hubbard

There is no substitute for hard work.

Thomas Edison

Diligence makes good luck.

Ben Franklin

Be like a postage stamp — stick to one thing
       till you get there.

Josh Billings

All-American Wisdom

It is easier to do a job right than to explain
      why you didn't.
                                 Martin Van Buren

The reward of a thing well done is to
      have done it.
                                Ralph Waldo Emerson

Do your work with your whole heart, and you
will succeed — there is so little competition.
                                 Elbert Hubbard

Whatever you do, do it with
      all your heart and soul.
                                 Bernard Baruch

Your Work

There is not only utility in labor,
>   but also beauty and dignity.
>> *Booker T. Washington*

To love what you do and feel that it matters —
>   how could anything else be more fun?
>> *Katharine Graham*

Believe in the Lord, and He
>   will do half the work — the last half.
>> *Cyrus Curtis*

17

Love and Forgiveness

The more we love, the more we can forgive, and the more we forgive, the more we can love. Love and forgiveness go hand in hand. One without the other is so fleeting.

Love and Forgiveness

Life is an exercise in forgiveness.

Norman Cousins

All-American Wisdom

Love ... the essence of God.
> *Ralph Waldo Emerson*

A man is as good as what he loves.
> *Saul Bellow*

Bitterness imprisons life; love releases it.
> *Harry Emerson Fosdick*

Forgiveness is the final form of love.
> *Reinhold Niebuhr*

Develop and maintain the capacity to forgive.
> *Martin Luther King, Jr.*

Love and Forgiveness

The first duty of love is to listen.

Paul Tillich

Folks never understand the folks they hate.

James Russell Lowell

The giving of love is an education in itself.

Eleanor Roosevelt

All-American Wisdom

Hating people is like burning down
    your own house to get rid of a rat.
                                Harry Emerson Fosdick

One of the most time consuming things
    is to have an enemy.
                                        E. B. White

Destroy your enemy by
    making friends with him.
                                        Abraham Lincoln

Love and Forgiveness

Love becomes help.
>   *Paul Tillich*

Peace is always beautiful.
>   *Walt Whitman*

Calmness is always Godlike.
>   *Ralph Waldo Emerson*

Peace, like charity, begins at home.
>   *Franklin D. Roosevelt*

If you would be loved, love and be lovable.
>   *Ben Franklin*

18

All-Purpose Advice

What follows is American advice for sensible living. Follow it and prosper.

All-Purpose Advice

Discourage litigation.

Abraham Lincoln

Vote for the man who promises the least.

Bernard Baruch

Expect the best.

Norman Vincent Peale

All-American Wisdom

In the long run, we hit only what we aim at. Aim high.

Henry David Thoreau

All-Purpose Advice

Discover creative solitude.
> *Carl Sandburg*

If you want a thing, go — if not, send.
> *Ben Franklin*

The misfortunes hardest to bear
are those that never come.
> *James Russell Lowell*

The trouble with most of us is that we'd rather be ruined by praise than saved by criticism.
> *Norman Vincent Peale*

All-American Wisdom

Anger blows out the lamp of the mind.
> *Robert Ingersoll*

Treat pain and rage as visitors.
> *Ben Hecht*

We are not punished for our sins,
but by them.
> *Elbert Hubbard*

All-Purpose Advice

Find the journey's end in every step.

Ralph Waldo Emerson

All-American Wisdom

See the miraculous in the commonplace.

Henry David Thoreau

All-Purpose Advice

Fill what's empty. Empty what's full. Scratch where it itches.

Alice Roosevelt Longworth

Sources

Sources

John Adams: President (1735-1826)
Lucille Ball: Comedienne (1911-1989)
Tallulah Bankhead: Actress (1902 - 1968)
P. T. Barnum: Showman (1810-1891)
John Barrymore: Actor (1882-1942)
Bernard Baruch: Financier (1870-1965)
Saul Bellow: Novelist (b. 1915)
Jack Benny: Comedian (1894-1974)
Irving Berlin: Songwriter (1888-1989)
Yogi Berra: Baseball Player and Coach (b. 1925)
Josh Billings: Auctioneer, Humorist (1818-1885)
Dorthea Brande: Editor, Author (1893-1948)
William Jennings Bryan: Statesman, Orator (1860-1925)
Eddie Cantor: Comedian (1892-1964)
Andrew Carnegie: Industrialist (1835-1919)
Dale Carnegie: Author (1888-1955)
Norman Cousins: Writer, Editor (1915-1990)
Davy Crockett: Frontiersman (1786-1836)
Cyrus Curtis: Publisher (1850-1933)
Elmer Davis: Journalist, Radio Personality (1890-1958)
Emily Dickinson: Poet (1830-1886)
Everett Dirksen: Statesman (1896-1969)
Thomas Edison: Inventor (1847-1931)
Dwight D. Eisenhower: General, President (1890-1969)
Ralph Waldo Emerson: Philosopher, Writer, Lecturer, (1803-1882)
Frederick Faust: Author (1892-1944)
Harvey Firestone, Jr.: Industrialist (1898-1973)
Henry Ford: Automotive Pioneer (1863-1947)

All-American Wisdom

Malcolm Forbes: Publisher (1919-1990)
Harry Emerson Fosdick: Clergyman, Author (1878-1969)
Ben Franklin: Statesman, Publisher, Author (1706-1790)
Robert Frost: Poet (1874-1963)
Samuel Goldwyn: Movie Executive (1882-1974)
Katharine Graham: Publisher (b. 1917)
Nathaniel Hawthorne: Author (1804-1964)
Ben Hecht: Writer (1893-1964)
Ernest Hemingway: Author (1899-1961)
Patrick Henry: Revolutionary Hero (1736-1799)
Oliver Wendell Holmes, Sr.: Physician, Author (1809-1894)
Oliver Wendell Holmes, Jr.: Supreme Court Justice (1841-1935)
Elbert Hubbard: Writer, Publisher (1856-1915)
Robert Ingersoll: Lecturer, Author (1833-1899)
Washington Irving: Novelist, Essayist (1783-1859)
Andrew Jackson: President (1767-1845)
Jesse Jackson: Civil Rights Leader, Clergyman (b. 1941)
William James: Psychologist (1842-1910)
Thomas Jefferson: President (1743-1826)
Janis Joplin: Singer (1943-1970)
E. Stanley Jones: Missionary, Author (1884-1973)
Henry J. Kaiser: Industrialist (1882-1967)
Helen Keller: Author, Lecturer, Advocate for the Handicapped (1880-1968)
Charles Kettering: Automotive Engineer, Executive, Inventor (1876-1958)

Sources

Martin Luther King, Jr.: Civil Rights Leader, Clergyman (1929-1968)
Ray Kroc: Industrialist, Fast Food Pioneer (1902-1984)
Robert E. Lee: Confederate General ((1807-1870)
Abraham Lincoln: President (1809-1865)
Anne Morrow Lindbergh: Author (b. 1906)
Walter Lippmann: Journalist, Author (1889-1974)
James Russell Lowell: Poet (1819-1891)
Alice Roosevelt Longworth: Author, Daughter of Teddy Roosevelt (1884-1980)
Douglas MacArthur: General (1880-1964)
Edgar Lee Masters: Poet, Novelist (1868-1950)
Herman Melville: Novelist, Poet (1819-1861)
Grandma Moses: Painter ((1860-1961)
Reinhold Niebuhr: Theologian, Author (1892-1971)
Thomas Paine: Author, Patriot (1737-1809)
George S. Patton: General (1885-1945)
Norman Vincent Peale: Clergyman, Author, Publisher (1898-1993)
Mary Pickford: Actress (1893-1979)
Eddie Rickenbacker: Airman, Hero, Executive (1890-1973)
Will Rogers: Humorist, Writer (1879-1935)
Eleanor Roosevelt: Author, First Lady (1884-1962)
Franklin D. Roosevelt: President (1882-1945)
Teddy Roosevelt: President (1858-1919)
Artur Rubinstein: Concert Pianist (1886-1982)
Babe Ruth: Baseball Legend and Home Run King (1895-1948)
Carl Sandburg: Poet, Biographer (1878-1967)

All-American Wisdom

George Santayana: Philosopher, Writer (1863-1952)
Robert Schuller: Reverend, Author
Charles M. Schwab: Industrialist (1862-1939)
Mack Sennett: Movie Executive (1884 - 1960)
B. F. Skinner: Psychologist, Author (1904-1990)
Alfred E. Smith: Governor of New York (1873-1944)
John Steinbeck: Author (1902-1968)
Gloria Steinem: Writer, Editor, Feminist (b. 1934)
Casey Stengel: Baseball Player and Manager (1890-1975)
Henry David Thoreau: Naturalist, Essayist, Author (1817-1872)
James Thurber: Humorist, Writer, Artist (1894-1974)
Paul Tillich: Theologian, Philosopher (1886-1965)
Mike Todd: Movie Producer (1907-1958)
Mark Twain: Author (1835-1910)
Martin Van Buren: President (1782-1862)
Amy Vanderbilt: Author (1908-1974)
Booker T. Washington: Educator, Author (1856-1915)
Thomas J. Watson: Industrialist, Pioneering Executive at I.B.M. (1874-1956)
Daniel Webster: Statesman (1782-1852)
Ida B. Wells: Civil Rights Advocate (1862-1931)
Mae West: Actress (1893-1980)
E. B. White: Author, Humorist, Essayist (1889-1985)
Walt Whitman: Poet (1819-1892)
Frank Lloyd Wright: Architect (1869-1959)

About the Author

Criswell Freeman is a Doctor of Clinical Psychology living in Nashville, Tennessee. He is the author of *When Life Throws You a Curveball, Hit It* and other books from WALNUT GROVE PRESS. He is also a published songwriter.